Little Wren's Surprise

by Joyce Mallery
illustrated by Deborah Colvin Borgo

Core Decodable 87

McGraw Hill Education

Bothell, WA • Chicago, IL • Columbus, OH • New York, NY

MHEonline.com

Send all inquiries to:
McGraw-Hill Education
8787 Orion Place
Columbus, OH 43240

ISBN: 978-0-02-143394-0
MHID: 0-02-143394-1

Printed in Canada.

9 10 11 12 KOD 24

One day, a wren family saw
a strange thing on the grass.

"What is it?" asked Dad.

He tried wriggling under it, but it was too big.

"Can you write with it?" asked Mom.
Mom rubbed it. It made no marks.

"Let's wrap it up," said Little Wren.

But the wrinkled paper was too small.

A girl came into the yard.
"Here's the wrench!" she yelled.
"Now we can fix my bike."

"We were wrong," said Little Wren.
"It is a thing to fix bikes!"